_____

_____

_____

_____

_____

*It is not the walls that make
the city, but the people who
live within them. The walls
of London may be battered,
but the spirit of the Londoner
stands resolute and undismayed.*

– George VI –

WHITE STAR PUBLISHERS

London, thou art the flower of cities all!
Gemme of all joy, jasper of jocunditie.

- William Dunbar -

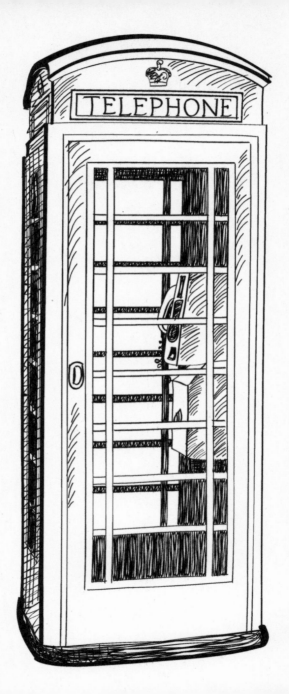

It is difficult to speak adequately
or justly of London. It is not
a pleasant place; it is not agreeable,
or cheerful, or easy, or exempt
from reproach. It is only magnificent.

- Henry James -

How sweet the morning air is!
See how that one little cloud floats
like a pink feather from some gigantic
flamingo. Now the red rim of the sun
pushes itself over the London
cloud-bank. It shines on a good
many folk, but on none, I dare bet,
who are on a stranger errand than
you and I. How small we feel with
our petty ambitions and strivings
in the presence of the great
elemental forces of Nature!

- Arthur Conan Doyle -

I have been interested in fashion since I was a kid. Then I lived in London, where it was more about costume and a personal statement of who you are than about fashion.

– Zaha Hadid –

There are two places in the world
where men can most effectively
disappear — the city of London
and the South Seas.

- Herman Melville -

A man who can dominate a London
dinner-table can dominate the world.
The future belongs to the dandy.
It is the exquisites
who are going to rule.

- Oscar Wilde -

My Dad says that being
a Londoner has nothing to do
with where you're born. He says
that there are people who get
off a jumbo jet at Heathrow,
go through immigration waving
any kind of passport, hop on the
tube and by the time the train's
pulled into Piccadilly Circus
they've become a Londoner.

— Ben Aaronovitch —

London is a paradise for the collector and the surface of this Eden of old and rare things stretches as far as the eye.

– Giorgio Porro –

The best bribe which London offers
today to the imagination, is that,
in such a vast variety of people and
conditions, one can believe there is room
for persons of romantic character to
exist, and that the poet, the mystic,
and the hero may hope to confront
their counterparts.

- Ralph Waldo Emerson -

There's nowhere
else like London.
Nothing at all, anywhere.

- Vivienne Westwood -

London is a modern Babylon.

- Benjamin Disraeli -

When I consider this great City in its several quarters and divisions, I look upon it as an aggregate of various nations, distinguished from each other by their respective customs, manners, and interests.

- Joseph Addison -

At present, people see fogs,
not because there are fogs,
but because poets and painters
have taught them the mysterious
loveliness of such effects.
There may have been fogs for
centuries in London. I dare say
there were. But no one saw them,
and so we do not know anything
about them. They did not exist
until Art had invented them.

- Oscar Wilde -

You find no man, at all intellectual, who is willing to leave London. No, Sir, when a man is tired of London, he is tired of life; for there is in London all that life can afford.

- Samuel Johnson -

The Thames was beautiful, dark,
and swift beneath the billion yellow
and white lights of the city . . .

- Charles Finch -

This is a London particular [...] A fog, miss.

– Charles Dickens –

He who has not seen it rain
in London, has not seen London.

- Edmondo De Amicis -

You will recognize,
my boy, the first sign
of old age: it is when
you go out into
the streets of London
and realize for the
first time how young
the policemen look

- Seymour Hicks -

London [...] is the largest city on Earth,
I thought - and that's a kind of absolute
no other city can achieve, since,
while there might be more beautiful cities,
with these one can never be certain
which one in particular is
the most beautiful.

- Edmondo De Amicis -

A mighty mass of brick,
and smoke, and shipping,
dirty and dusty, but as wide as eye
could reach, with here
and there a sail just skipping
in sight, then lost amidst the forestry
of masts; a wilderness of steeples peeping
on tiptoe through their sea-coal canopy;
a huge, dun cupola, like a foolscap crown
on a fool's head - and there is
London Town.

- Lord Byron -

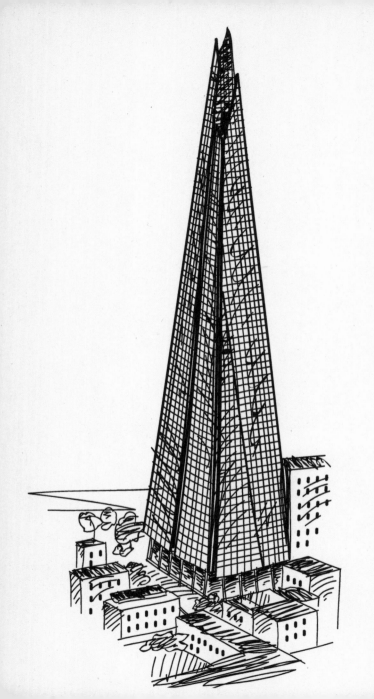

London is too full of fogs
and serious people. Whether the
fogs produce the serious people,
or whether the serious people
produce the fogs, I don't know.

- Oscar Wilde -

In people's eyes, in the swing, tramp,
and trudge; in the bellow and the uproar;
the carriages, motor cars, omnibuses, vans,
sandwich men shuffling and swinging;
brass bands; barrel organs; in the triumph
and the jingle and the strange high singing
of some aeroplane overhead was
what she loved; life; London;
this moment of June.

– Virginia Woolf –

London – beautiful, immortal
London – has never been a 'city'
in the simplest sense of the word.
It was, and is, a living, breathing
thing, a stone leviathan that harbours
secrets underneath its scales.
It guards them covetously, hiding
them deep within its body; only
the mad or the worthy can find them.

– Samantha Shannon –

I wandered thro' each charter'd street,
near where the charter'd Thames does flow.
And mark in every face I meet,
marks of weakness, marks of woe.

- William Blake -

I have seen the most remarkable
phenomenon that the world
has to show to the amazed
mind of man. I have seen it
and I am still amazed. In my
memory there remains the stone
forest of houses and in between
the surging stream of vivid
human faces, with all their gay
passions, with all their horrible
flurry of love and hunger
and hate — I mean London.

— Henrich Heine —

Aaronovitch, Ben, *1964-, English writer*

Addison, Joseph, *1672-1719, English politician, writer and dramatist*

Blake, William, *1757-1827, English poet, carver and painter*

De Amicis, Edmondo, *1846-1908, Italian writer and journalist*

Dickens, Charles, *1812-1870, English writer, journalist and travel reporter*

Disraeli, Benjamin, *1804-1881, English politician and writer*

Doyle, Arthur Conan, *1859-1930, Scottish writer*

Dunbar, William, *1459-1530, Scottish poet*

Emerson, Ralph Waldo, *1803-1882, American philosopher, writer and essayist*

Finch, Charles, *1980-, American writer and literary critic*

George VI, *1895-1952, King of the United Kingdom*

Hadid, Zaha, *1950-2016, Iraqi-born British architect and designer*

Heine, Henrich, *1797-1856, German poet*

Hicks, Seymour, *1871-1949, English actor and filmmaker*

James, Henry, *1843-1916, American writer and literary critic*

Johnson, Samuel, *1709-1784, English literary critic, poet and essayist*

Lord Byron, *1788-1824, English poet and politician*

Melville, Herman, *1819-1891, American writer, poet and literary critic*

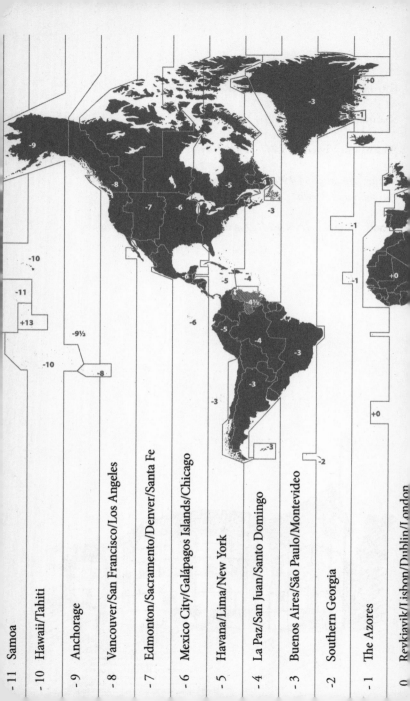

- 11 Samoa
- 10 Hawaii/Tahiti
- 9 Anchorage
- 8 Vancouver/San Francisco/Los Angeles
- 7 Edmonton/Sacramento/Denver/Santa Fe
- 6 Mexico City/Galápagos Islands/Chicago
- 5 Havana/Lima/New York
- 4 La Paz/San Juan/Santo Domingo
- 3 Buenos Aires/São Paulo/Montevideo
- 2 Southern Georgia
- 1 The Azores
0 Reykjavik/Lisbon/Dublin/London

TIME ZONES

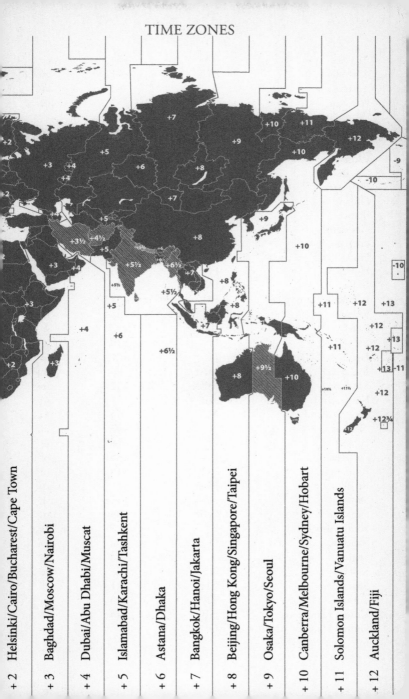

+ 2 Helsinki/Cairo/Bucharest/Cape Town

+ 3 Baghdad/Moscow/Nairobi

+ 4 Dubai/Abu Dhabi/Muscat

+ 5 Islamabad/Karachi/Tashkent

+ 6 Astana/Dhaka

+ 7 Bangkok/Hanoi/Jakarta

+ 8 Beijing/Hong Kong/Singapore/Taipei

+ 9 Osaka/Tokyo/Seoul

+ 10 Canberra/Melbourne/Sydney/Hobart

+ 11 Solomon Islands/Vanuatu Islands

+ 12 Auckland/Fiji

LICENSE PLATES, AREA CODES, DOMAINS,

Argentina	RA	+54	.ar
Australia	AUS	+61	.au
Austria	A	+43	.at
Belgium	B	+32	.be
Brazil	BR	+55	.br
Canada	CDN	+1	.ca
China	CN	+86	.cn
Croatia	HR	+385	.hr
Denmark	DK	+45	.dk
Finland	FIN	+358	.fi
France	F	+33	.fr
Germany	D	+49	.de
Greece	GR	+30	.gr
Hong Kong	HK	+852	.hk
Hungary	H	+36	.hu
India	IND	+91	.in
Ireland	IRL	+353	.ie
Iceland	IS	+354	.is
Israel	IL	+972	.il
Italy	I	+39	.it
Japan	J	+81	.jp
Malaysia	MAL	+60	.my
Mexico	MEX	+52	.mx
Netherlands	NL	+31	.nl
New Zealand	NZ	+64	.nz
Norway	N	+47	.no
Poland	PL	+48	.pl
Portugal	P	+351	.pt
Romania	RO	+40	.ro
Russia	RUS	+7	.ru
Slovakia	SK	+421	.sk
Slovenia	SLO	+386	.si
South Africa	ZA	+27	.za
South Korea	ROK	+82	.kr
Spain	E	+34	.es
Sweden	S	+46	.se
Switzerland	CH	+41	.ch
Turkey	TR	+90	.tr
United Kingdom	GB	+44	.uk
United States of America	USA	+1	.us

LANGUAGES AND CURRENCY

Spanish	Argentine peso
English	Australian dollar
German	Euro
French (Walloon), Dutch (Flemish) and German	Euro
Portuguese	Brazilian real
English and French	Canadian dollar
Chinese	Chinese renminbi
Croatian	Croatian kuna
Danish	Danish krone
Finnish and Swedish	Euro
French	Euro
German	Euro
Greek	Euro
Chinese and English	Hong Kong dollar
Hungarian	Hungarian Forint
Hindi and English	Indian rupee
Irish Gaelic and English	Euro
Icelandic	Icelandic króna
Hebrew and Arabic	New shekel
Italian	Euro
Japanese	Japanese yen
Malay	Malaysian ringgit
Spanish	Mexican peso
Dutch and Frisian	Euro
English and Māori	New Zealand dollar
Norwegian	Norwegian krone
Polish	Polish złoty
Portuguese	Euro
Romanian	Romanian leu
Russian	Russian ruble
Slovak	Euro
Slovene, Italian and Hungarian	Euro
English and Afrikaans	South African rand
Korean South	Korean won
Spanish	Euro
Swedish	Swedish krona
German, French, Italian and Romansh	Swiss franc
Turkish	New Turkish lira
English	Pound sterling
English	United States dollar

Men

Shirts

USA	14½	15	15½	16	16½	17
GB	14½	15	15½	16	16½	17
D	37	38	39	40	41	42
F	37	38	39	40	41	42
I	37	38	39	40	41	42

Suits/Coats

USA	36	38	40	42	44	46
GB	36	38	40	42	44	46
D	40	42	44	46	48	50
F	42	44	46	48	50	52
I	46	48	50	52	54	56

Jeans

USA	32	33	34	35	36	38
GB	32	33	34	35	36	38
D	32	33	34	35	36	38
F	32	33	34	35	36	38
I	32	33	34	35	36	38

Shoes

USA	8½	9	9½	10	10½	11
GB	8	8½	9	9½	10	10½
D	40	41	42	43	44	45
F	40	41	42	43	44	45
I	40	41	42	43	44	45

Length

1 in = 2.54 cm
0.3937 in = 1 cm
1 SM = 1.6093 km
0.6214 SM = 1 km
1 NM = 1.8519 km
0.5400 NM = 1 km

Area

1 ac = 0.4047 ha
2.471 ac = 1 ha
1 SM^2 = 2.5900 km^2
0.3861 SM^2 = 1 km^2

SIZES, MEASUREMENTS AND CONVERSIONS

Women

Shirts

USA	4	6	8	10	12	14
GB	6	8	10	12	14	16
D	32	34	36	38	40	42
F	34	36	38	40	42	44
I	38	40	42	44	46	48

Dresses/Suits

USA	4	6	8	10	12	14
GB	6	8	10	12	14	16
D	32	34	36	38	40	42
F	34	36	38	40	42	44
I	38	40	42	44	46	48

Jeans

USA	4	6	6-8	8-10	10	12
GB	25	27	28	29	30	32
D	25	27	28	29	30	32
F	25	27	28	29	30	32
I	25	27	28	29	30	32

Shoes

USA	6	6½	7½	8½	9	9½
GB	3½	4	5	6	6½	7
D	36	37	38	39	40	41
F	35	36	37	38	39	40
I	36	37	38	39	40	41

Weight
1 oz = 28.349 g
1 g = 0.03527 oz
1 lb = 0.4536 kg
1 kg = 2.205 lb

Volume
1 (USA) gal = 3.7854 l
0.2642 (USA) gal = 1 l
1 (GB) gal = 4.5460 l
0.2200 (GB) gal = 1 l

Temperature
0 °C = 32 °F

Speed
1 mph = 1.6 km/h

Illustrated by
Marisa Vestita

Graphic design
Valentina Giammarinaro

WHITE STAR PUBLISHERS

WS White Star Publishers® is a registered trademark
property of White Star s.r.l.

© 2017 White Star s.r.l.
Piazzale Luigi Cadorna, 6
20123 Milan, Italy
www.whitestar.it

Translation: Iceigeo, Milan

ISBN 978-88-544-1118-0
1 2 3 4 5 6   21 20 19 18 17

Printed in Italy by Rotolito Lombarda - Seggiano di Pioltello (MI)